GOD
Does Not Sucker Punch!

~A Scatterbrain's Path to God~

PEPPY POPPET

Fulton Books
Meadville, PA

Published by Fulton Books 2024

ISBN 979-8-88731-358-0 (paperback)
ISBN 979-8-88731-359-7 (digital)

Printed in the United States of America

If you read this with the right mindset, you will sail through this millennium in a state of bliss.

With this book, you'll get my life experience through seven quick chapters and then in chapter 8, you will get 11 11 44 44, which adds up to 110.

To value something more than yourself is the key to getting a leg up the ladder to heaven. But for a scatterbrain such as myself, the lesson was mostly about—a place for everything and everything in its place and then to recapture the presence of mind that came along with it.

CONTENTS

CHAPTER 1

THE BEGINNING

My dad liked to create a frenzy of activity. We were given a badminton racket, a tennis racket, and a ping-pong bat in the same week. As a result, we were supposed to excel in all three games although the wristwork required to play ping-pong was in direct opposition with the broad strokes needed to play tennis or the velocity required to hit the shuttlecock. This frenzied approach to sports became the foundation stone, the underlying paradigm in all the other categories of my life, especially because my parents were polar opposites in their approach to raising children, and they both wanted to have an equal say in how we were raised.

So it appears that I was raised to be a scatterbrain, but here was what I did that amplified it. I thought I was operating as a gregarious Aquarius that gave me the impetus to get involved in everything that caught my attention. Just to give you an idea of my diverse set of activities—I participated in paratrooping, modeling, gliding, ping-pong, and first aid all in the same time period. And I got involved in ballroom dancing, sketching, as well as cooking, baking, flower arrangement, and French classes all within the same day. My itinerary was similar to that of perpetual tourists who have several tour guides, giving them the life experience at diverse venues.

I was born in the Year of the Dog, which makes me honest, intelligent, straightforward, and loyal with a sense of justice and fair play. However, the same cannot be said about many key people in my rolodex.

From the time I was little, I wanted to be swept into mystical, mythological worlds. I definitely craved the paranormal. *The Magic Faraway Tree* by Enid Blyton (in recent times, I found out that the name Enid is synonymous with Eden, and Eden is where God's presence is legendary) was fantastic to read, as were its spin-offs. And if there was any chance that the tall trees at the apartment complex at VRC Road in Madras, India, could connect and tune in to the higher vibrations, then that was all I would have done day and night—climb those tall trees. I would have ignored ping-pong and playing scrabble altogether.

Does the earth have hidden vortexes that then become our portals? I strongly feel there are small ones, everywhere. The big ones are hard to find because they probably got dissipated by disgruntled rejects who felt snubbed by the spirit world.

Anyway, pretty soon after I moved to Madras, I got into trouble with my second grade teacher and then my fourth grade teacher, who was incredibly draconian. In short, she and many others disrespected my sweetness. And that was when I began to seriously comprehend that to defeat the evil eye that tries to dissipate souls, well, I would just have to be on point 24/7, 365 days a year. And right then, I didn't have the wherewithal to do that because my mother was a working mom and my dad only put in appearances periodically. So it was mostly an absentee dad situation. And the maidservant was pretty harsh when it came to her interaction with me, but she perpetually used her housekeeping duties to justify her hostile attitude toward me. It was at that point in my life that I seriously started to live in my fantasy world any time I wasn't actively playing at a sport.

Although it was calming to live in my fantasy world, I soon got labeled as a daydreamer and got in further trouble for that. But I didn't stop trying to blend in academically at school, as well as in sports after school. And if many chose to think that I was too childlike, then that was their choice. Needless to say, I was quite heavily criticized for being authentic to my soul instead of being a traditional girl. So my scattered life was a myriad of exciting experiences and horrible scenes of betrayal too.

As an exuberant youngster, I was often caught off guard when some mean-spirited people would engage me in animated conversations, then drain me of all my information, and walk away after making some sarcastic remark, which left a sour note in the air. I would often be bewildered at the expertise with which they dissipated my loving aura and enthusiasm. And I just knew that if I had a protective big sister, or maybe if I'd been given a protective amulet or some special crystals to wear, then perhaps I might have fared better. But I was not lucky in my support group, and so I grew up without any psychic protection or armor. As a result, most people were able to get into my head in moments!

This all-out attack on my individuality and tentative sexuality began instantaneously because most of my life played out in public. The clubs, the schools, the neighborhood kids, and the beaches were very much a part of my waking life. Strangely, I was even on display as I slept because we had big windows in our bedroom, and our apartment was the first one by the gate. And so it turned out, my life's crucial milestones and my getting to them were often based on coin tosses of anyone and everyone who seemed to have in-depth knowledge about me. Sadly, most people I grew up with were class

A manipulators and certainly not for the betterment of any party involved. They were just troublemakers who excelled in breaking anyone's potential.

Over the years, as I began to progress my life, moving from zip code to zip code, city to city, state to state, I understood that people around me were absorbing big chunks of my soul's energy, lots of it; and each time I moved, I felt like I had to start from scratch, even in my behavior patterns.

In recent times, I decided that I would put together everything I really valued in my daily routine into a manual, so no matter where I moved to, I would be able to function optimally within forty-eight hours of getting there, even if there were strong hellish spells to heighten the chaotic energy about me. I do believe we hit false notes in situations only if we did not prepare for it. So I always reminded myself to be prepared to do a 180 if there was bad, deadbeat energy somewhere. And one task at a time, with the right music, was optimal.

Mostly, I make my policy known: anyone who has electronically tormented me, be it male or female, if they've ambushed and sabotaged me, well they can't rise in any way unless they encounter the very same challenging milestones of my life and then they outdo my batting average. And they'll have to deal with many more hardships than mine, just to make up for that element of surprise, because it's about reversing their own test paradigm on them but in a heightened way. Mainly because they have been saboteurs for so long that they know every angle of any challenge, and so we will have to amp up the hardships reserved for them.

Personally, most people will agree that I am fun-loving, dramatic, passionate, generous, and creative. And once I make a choice, I do not give up easily because if I've actually made a choice, then I want to be sure that I live up to the potential of that choice. Therefore, if some say that I have been obstinate, please know that they are basically projecting their own obstinacy onto me. It is important to note that my decisions and actions do not include criminal behavior. Also, I am just somebody who's totally into ethics. I certainly believe that even if your morals are lacking but if you have some ethics, I could still connect with you, especially if you are consistent within the framework of your meagre ethics and values.

It is crucial to note that all through my formative years, the message I got was: life was about being rough 'n' tough, about roughing it out. And at some point, when the education was completed and a good job was attained, then the right man might appear. Until then, sexing men was out of the question. Sex was not a necessity. It was work ethic that mattered.

Now we all know that most people if put into a particular circumstance will conform. So to this day, I am not sure exactly how my life would have turned out if I had been inducted into men's world as a prospective sex partner from the get-go. But then, India would not have been able to create a revolution around me—the revolution to resort to vagrant behavior and colossal damage just to make sure that they are doing whatever it takes to induct me sexually and to make sure that I will be given a sex education although everybody knows that I made sure to use the internet and incisive questioning to gain a better handle on the different aspects of sex! However, most people do admit that sex education through a demonstration of a role-play-type intercourse by mature adults while I was in the eighth grade would have sufficed. But if a demonstration of sexual intercourse had been scheduled for my benefit in the eighth grade, then how could the deviant Indians have been able to justify their revolution, their attacking the prestigious institutions of the White world, the way they have been able to do so currently?

Finally, it is common knowledge that the evil eye was put on me even before I completed my first few months of life in India.

ASSORTED DEMONS

(With stellar heart and affirmations in verses,
I sure can turn around hexes and curses.
As these intentions of mine are spoken,
I am certain the evil spells at me are broken.)

My personal experience had taught me this: if a spell had been placed
on some action you do, then do it in reverse, in a bottoms-up way.
For instance, my maid in India, by the name of Jaya, oftentimes

tugged at my hair in a way so that she could make it snap and break while braiding it. At some point in time, when I got a shorter haircut, she resented the fact that I didn't need her to braid my hair anymore, well at least for a while.

Then when my hair grew long again, I decided to braid my hair myself. Strangely, I found it hard to braid my own hair the traditional way. It was almost as if somebody was opposing me with every twist and turn of the braid when I braided my hair the traditional way. However, when I braided my hair in the reverse direction, I managed just fine, although the top part of the braid stuck out. So using reverse braiding, I was able to get past the obstacle, the freeze, and the spell that were placed on my hair, and then I began to braid away.

To trash a powerful demon, you have to be a substantial entity from the light. Because first, the demon takes over the house and then the person living there. That is why, the moment I was able to, I filled my apartment with cute stuffed toys because they spread upbeat, playful energy that was closer to my soul essence. And when you fill your space with energy that's close to your own soul's energy, then that's like saying to the demon, "Demon, you have no hold over me. You have no power here."

I do believe that if you wrongly unleash any demon, even a karma demon, then it'll stalk you right back. It follows that some of my so-called relatives and the maidservants, as well as some neighbors and peers, who had schemed and put *drishti* or evil eye on me found that they encountered bigger challenges and obstacles in their lives as a result of their wayward behavior. I also noticed that many flight attendants who ganged up against me, with the idea of putting me down based on their behind-the-scenes tryst with my troublemaker maid Radha's minions, had major turmoil in their lives. As things turned out, at some point they encountered real bad luck in their personal lives and premeditatively decided to become my staunch enemies instead of reflecting upon their own choices and decisions.

It is no secret that I have been known to suggest menial and manual labor for hard core, repeat offender deviants. I have repeatedly advocated that their punishment should be designed in the form of a yoke on their deviant bull necks, as opposed to terminating them. The reason is simple—when they die, they may return as dirty, vicious spirits or even a ghost, and I do not want to get ambushed by ghostly stalkers. I can barely tolerate the stalkers who are currently in their physical bodies!

It is true when they say black magic strikes fear in your heart, and you need every bit of light to fight it. In other words, you have to have your secret magic to match it—perhaps white magic! I do believe that I was the target of a specific witch hunt because I'm a combination of athlete, scholar, fool, and virgin. But that also meant that although death is stalking me, it might first massacre the whores. Simply because although in the past, whores were more easily subjugated, however, in recent times, they have become extremely toxic while I am just looking to retire completely. So now it appears that the whores will have to be put down before I am put to sleep. Especially because their toxicity has become an epidemic, and their mutiny, in large numbers, certainly harmed American society.

History tends to repeat itself unless we put in a better system of checks and balances. And we definitely don't want this Salem witch hunt paradigm to be allowed to escalate. Given the gender politics of Salem witch hunt time period, it's very important to note that then the women who were outspoken didn't fit in and were usually hunted. *But* I really wasn't one of the outspoken ones until it was decided that I had to be made to sound that way just so people could justify they were targeting me. Mainly because their original and follow-up accusations came from malicious treachery.

But I did do myself a favor though. By turning to stand-up comedy eighteen years ago, I got to be outspoken, without bitterness, because humor is what makes it stand-up comedy. And the more you mock yourself, the quicker you heal. Because you'll always know just how much to mock yourself and where at, that is if you're in touch with your inner child.

It is often said—the good Lord takes care of fools and drunks. Luckily, a comic/joker is considered to be *le fou*—the fool. So this meant that I had a fighting chance. Because if a whore who is corrupt and as a result, is scheduled to die first, then maybe I had bought myself some time by becoming a comic. *Unless* it's the other way around where a corrupt whore is considered more useful than me, and so I'm put to sleep first! But if the whore's word is not her bond, then how do you know that she will be available to anyone that asks once she has accomplished her hateful mission—rubbing me out.

So I had decided to stay alive through this high-tech lynching mainly because I had an innate desire to be better informed no matter what the venue. Especially because many of my supposed peers wanted for me to be swamped by the portals of hell and engineered that by continually messing with me through third parties. Some television celebrities even put a clamp on my astral projections for fear that I might travel too far. Maybe they felt that in a world of darkness filled with tortured souls on the astral plane, I might be in danger? Especially because my housemates and landlords seemed to crave a chance to possess my body while I was sleeping soundly. So preventing me from astral traveling might have seemed the only way to protect me?

To be honest, I am in no hurry to astral travel, at least not until I get to Nome, western Alaska. I am happy to read about it though. And if it occurs naturally, then so be it. But I shall not pursue astral travel until I get to western Alaska.

It is widely known that witches are dependent upon the dead for their livelihood. Coincidentally, throughout this witch hunt on me, because I was consistently praying to the heavenly entities and my dead ancestors as they were my only support group then, people conveniently thought they could classify me as a witch! Especially because I was friendly with diverse cross sections of personality types then.

Yes, I was the type of person who wanted to have friends from all walks of life because I really believed that opposites balanced us. And certainly, I would have liked to have been invited to even watch different rituals without participating because I didn't condemn or exalt witchery. And no, I did not; and even now, I do not think that I'm the only one with a deep connection to God.

They say it's hard for a witch to shed a tear or blush. As a comic, I wondered if my dictum to never shed a tear would further classify me as a witch. *Would I then be expected to hum to a cat on a rug or after placing the cat on my lap? Would I also be expected to live by dark magic?* So far, I have stuck to staying in the light. For some reason, I chose to be closer to the forces of (mother) nature to a point where I began listening to the thunder and watching the lightning, the rain and trying to figure out what the different seasons seemed to say. Also, sunrises and sunsets seemed to be another portal into the cosmic blueprint. In addition, I also decided that I'd let numerology and astrology do their bit in nudging me especially because I am blessed with very strong numbers and two cool stelliums.

A quick final paragraph on demonic possession and its impact on my witch hunt. So it appears there are high-level and low-level demons. And when I was routinely targeted/attacked, I decided that it could become my mission to make sure that hard-core evildoers are sent to the lowest depths of the hellish plane. Mainly because they wouldn't stop targeting me. Especially because once they had figured that I wasn't going to commit suicide, they acted like they were justifiably outraged when they were not!

However, I knew I was true to what I said. Based on the relentless witch hunt on me, I had been emphatic in 2019 that I should ceremoniously be put to sleep in front of the whole world. I also clearly stated that there wasn't enough time for me to settle my affairs in order unless I got a hundred totally peaceful days where I was not targeted and instead left to peacefully go through my stuff. And to this day, that agitational targeting has not stopped, and I still jump out of my skin all through the day even as I superficially go through some of my stuff.

It has been my experience that if hell's portals are opened up by unscrupulous witches, then every few minutes seem like a lifetime, and there's a looping syndrome—where you feel like you're chasing your own tail so to speak. Almost as if you are a flaky-headed Pomeranian dog. An example of this looping syndrome happened when Peggy Burby's mean-spirited attitude on my confirmation flight as flight attendant seemed to cause the darkness, the impending doom, and the looping in midair. And I couldn't seem to appeal to her human side. Ditto for several different times when Mukesh Jhangiani, a devious Air India flight attendant, made sure that he said spells that caused a hellish change of atmosphere. He even expertly created a chaos situation that made me leave my Anand Mahal B-5 apartment key with a long red string attached to it in my front door lock and walk away, not once but twice in the same month. Now if that's not a recipe for theft, then what is?

Now currently those who are still targeting me, well they've to understand—they just have to un-indoctrinate themselves. And they have to untarget me because I can't wait to cleanse spiritually, to literally scrub all their bad spirits off me and get cleaned up, so I can share my pearls of wisdom with the world and hopefully not from a stretcher or the ICU.

Anyway, after arriving to the conclusion that these die hard—hard-core deviants were not people that you ever do deals with because their word wasn't their bond; well I have indefinitely postponed my ceremonious exit from this world until I am well settled in western Alaska, by the Bering Sea. I will let nature take its course once I am by the Bering Sea.

The ability to invoke a demon is fairly simple I am told. Just get a book of spells and follow the instructions. But the downside is that you could get stuck on this planet indefinitely if you invoke questionable entities and dark spirits. So it's best to work with the light if you are from the light as I am.

CHAPTER 3

THE KUGAAR CRUCIFIXION

According to the Egyptians, *Kugaar* is a place where they kill the soul slowly over fifteen years. In October 2001, Murray Yosha repeatedly spoke about a slow and painful death until I began to understand that he was referring to me. In terms of the paradigm being used at me especially because he certainly brought it up emphatically in a high-pitched voice, which made me look at him a little sharp. Yes, the Kugaar crucifixion that was aimed at me was one of the worst kept secrets of Hollywood and Vegas.

It is important to remember that evil exists in many forms. To keep your environment free from the dark side and its intent to do a possession, you should have certain objects in your environment that are indicative of the presence of light. People who are into wood and cleanliness are not possessed by evil spirits easily unless they consume alcohol, drugs or invoke evil spirits. And when you are possessed by an evil spirit, your heart is heavy, and you can't go to heaven unless you find a way to cleanse your soul, maybe through traveling to new places so you can break the hex and get rid of evil spirits.

Now how exactly did I end up with a "for religious persecution" target on my back? Well I seemed to make unusual choices that propelled me and my life to show up conspicuously on the radar of several powerful people, and quite unwittingly, I became a useful pawn to them. In addition, it soon became clear that I didn't exploit situations, and that endearing quality of mine became the reason for my longevity.

So, apparently Dharma is a son of Brahma, the Hindu god of creation. Allegedly, the resentful deviants of India took a dislike to me because they felt that Brahma might have been benevolent to me because I'm very duty-bound and respect education (goddess Saraswati is his consort).

As I focused on the reflections of my early life, I began to see and understand how a set of events that took place after I moved to the United States were from a cause set in motion in India, at the Hindu pilgrimage sites. And that pinpoints how it all started.

In my case, because I was a good child and a good teenager, my visiting different countries seemed to go well, and it was well-noticed that their deities, their demigods, their entities took a liking to me. And the outcome of my actions mostly came out okay, especially because my soul was easy to read. People also had this figured out— that I hadn't changed anything about my value system fundamentally, although my appearance, in terms of my hair and clothing, underwent many transformations.

So over the last four and a half decades, I read several books and articles in most categories—palmistry, astrology, numerology, mythology of different deities of many countries that I had visited and also of countries that I never visited. I certainly had the good fortune to travel extensively across five continents. And this happened during my formative and impressionable years. Particularly because I was an avid cable television watcher and I had jotted down immense amounts of notes on esoteric subject matters as well as of shows focusing on creating a better lifestyle. So I'll quickly sum up my understanding of some of the norms and practices in this world.

Muslims pray five times a day and facing Mecca is the key to heaven as is the thirty days of fasting for Ramadan from sunrise to sunset. Cannon blasts can mark the moment of sundown.

The concept of a violent end of the world is very prevalent. It is bandied about that the sons of light shall battle the sons of darkness. The Dead Sea Scrolls also deal with this.

Zoroastrians also believe that to eradicate evil, we have to have a cataclysmic battle. They believe in cleansing through fire.

Interesting to note—the Buddhists do not believe in Judgment Day or in absolute endings. They believe that people want to be free from oppression. Enlightenment is used to unveil truths. Truth is sometimes revealed through meditation and reflection. *Buddha* actually means the enlightened one. The point of Buddhism: we are all capable of more than what we are. And to detach from the material world is the equivalent of the end of suffering. In Chinese religion, everything has a reason. The five no-no's of Buddhism are: violence, stealing, sexual misconduct, lying or gossip, and intoxicating drugs/drinks/substance abuse.

Daoism—where gods are not the focus but interconnectedness is. And it is believed that our fates are all set at birth. Therefore, our life's map is to know where 120 stars were located at the time of our birth, which equals to our fate.

The Christian concept is that it is a single divine being who creates and governs the universe. The Vatican believes that miracles can turn people into saints! Jewish religion was built on a bedrock of divine intervention. The book of Revelations is a political and symbolic book.

So apparently Moses saw God in a bush. Muhammad hung around the mountain. Buddha attained enlightenment under a tree. And Muhammad actually went to heaven.

Also, the Mount of Olives, Wailing Wall, Temple Mount, and Herodian stones are famous venues leading to deep connections.

Day of the Dead in New Orleans is used to share food and beverage, music and candlelight with the dead.

Mayans believe floods eventually lead to an enduring afterlife. The Aztecs worshipped Inca gods that controlled rain. The Greek gods were kept busy by screwing each other over while their followers got painfully stuck in perilous situations. Hebrews waited for the Messiah who showed up but then the debate got split between Judaism and Christianity. However, although Muhammad got the Quran from Allah, he is not considered the final prophet by the Muslims.

In India, you pick gods based on their being a family deity or based on an emergency. Ganesha is considered a young god who removes obstacles. In addition, Hindus believe that the source of evil comes from unhappy souls of their ancestors. However, correct rituals liberate the unhappy souls. Only if the spirits of parents are not settled, then bad dreams can occur. And exorcisms happen from head to feet.

The Egyptians believe that the mummy was where the soul resided in its afterlife. They also buried their dead on the West Bank although they lived on the East Bank. And in 1922, King Tut's tomb was discovered with his treasures intact. Egyptians also believe that god Osiris is the god of the underworld and judges the weight of your heart. *The* heart is weighed against the goddess of truth, Maat, while Thot, her husband, writes down the judgment.

The seven deadly sins as we know them in the Christian world: wrath, gluttony, pride, greed, sloth, lust, and envy.

At this point, I need to mention that I was also nudged into getting into the realm of Quan Yin, who is like Mother Mary, in the Eastern world. I even spent a little time at the Hsi Lai Temple in Hacienda Heights, California, and other temples of that nature because I wanted to explore what Quan Yin, as a divine entity, wanted or had in store for me. However, my life's journey has lifted me directly into the realm of God Almighty, and the imagery in my mind is that of pop art version of the classical heavenly world that symbolizes to me the ruler of the galaxies. And I also do believe that 110 is a number that's close to God. That is why, as a Girl Scout, that number 110 saved me from so many mishaps.

My good fortune also led me to study the esoteric beliefs of numerous and diverse demographics. Owls are harbingers of death. Ghosts don't sleep or go to the bathroom. Northern lights in the Arctic Circle occur every December through March when charged particles from the sun hit atoms in earth's atmosphere and releases photons. Jews are 125 levels below God. Druids and Celts became Christian based on abject survivorhood. Halloween—where goblins and vampires realize what cultural approximation really is. Then there is the imagery of trident in hand while saying, "Rise, Atlantis." *Feng* means wind, and *shui* means water. And for things to flow smoothly, feng shui is necessary to harness it to our advantage. Then I found out on the internet that the four daughters of God are truth, righteous justice, mercy, and peace. Mercury is god of thievery. Concord equals harmony.

Then there are gods that bring people rain. Gods that bring war-victory, and gods of wine and song. And Romans believed that God controlled even their sporting event's outcome.

I also read about how the soul resides in the lungs or in the heart or brain or pineal gland. And the soul is yours as it is self-centered but the spirit belongs to God.

Also, there are some evidence that better witches have professional ethics, and so some covens actually do have a better assembly of witches.

Finally, I acknowledge that God masterfully governs the changing moments in our lives and steers us to safety if we indeed do place our hand in God's hand. However, I have to confess that anything I build with God's protection, well the deviants tend to rip it to shreds. That is why I understand that the deviants do need to be in sync with US laws because they're just too volatile. And I need to go back to God because I am a minority in terms of my moral character. So to the deviants I say, "You're insulting this country, and you've only been here for a short while."

There's another aspect to the deviants that I want to address, and this is to their credit. The deviants seemed to want to learn my philosophy to life and literally inhaled 11 11 44 44 even as I wrote it and submitted it on the internet.

CHAPTER 4

RUNNING THROUGH A WIND TUNNEL

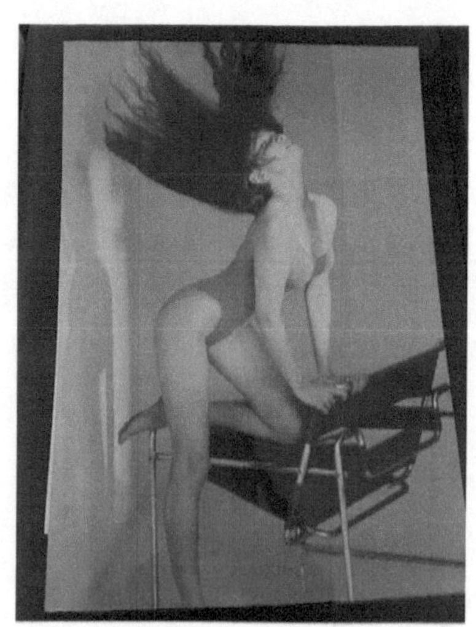

Now if your throat, jaw, and rib cage, as well as shoulder blades, are hit with reverse polarity and agitation, then that assault is a good entry point for any demon to torment you. Luckily, I was able to volley some of the torment sent my way, by putting out more exposes.

So I would feverishly start jotting down notes or directly use my android to put out my posts and tweets, and in recent times, even do my podcasts just so I could harness my tormented energy, at least some of it, without it totally going to waste. However, the difference between my reflective posts (which are usually written when I am at peace with myself) and my tortured posts is pretty obvious, especially in the language that flies out of my tweets and posts while I am battling demons.

What I'd inferred from reading several articles and books on demons is—they don't like open combat. So if you just look busy, and keep your head down, and especially if you do tedious activities for prolonged periods of time, then mostly, the demons do go away. Unless, of course, somebody really evil has called in the *devastation demon* that wakes up and comes out once every one thousand years and feels compelled to create quite a dramatic-topple-impact effect! So oftentimes, when deviants/players ask for and are granted an extra thirty days, I optimistically think that maybe they're trying to turn over a new leaf. It usually is because they're asking their demonic entity for those extra thirty days just to beat down harder on some contender who is a jewel of society!

Mainly, from browsing through countless books and cult movies, I comprehended what the dark strategy was—possession in stages. Stage one: infestation—where you sense that there are spirits whispering and making their presence felt. Infestation is the time to get help immediately or move out so you can avoid a head-on collision with the dark side. Stage two: oppression—where the spirits find a vulnerable person and start bullying that person. Oppression is serious, and if you don't make a noise about it, it will progress to where there is possession.

Folks, I think by now the whole world is aware of the big noise I made when the infestation and oppression were aimed at me. And only through raising awareness was I able to create a mini fortress and shake off stage three—which is very hard to shake off as it is a full-blown possession. One of the main reasons why my exposes were so detailed, and why I kept hitting home runs as an activist, is because my exposes were my only ammunition against the dark side. And now the whole world is watchful of my precariously balanced life. Because the word is out that every quack and charlatan is being allowed to unleash their darkness and demons on me and watch to see if I can fight it off. So my anguish and torment have become a sport for people to watch.

Now it is globally known that the order of the ten curses that visited upon the Pharaohs before Exodus for holding the Jews as slaves are the following:

1. boils,
2. bats,
3. frogs,
4. blood,
5. rats,
6. hail,
7. beasts,
8. locusts,
9. the death of the first born, and
10. darkness.

And to dramatize their targeting of me, in a sickeningly melo-dramatic way, the deviants of India chose to aim lasers and zingers and flares at different parts of my body with increasing velocity and amplitude so as to damage my tissues and create a "chronic" ill health situation. So they initially pretended that I had done them wrong (when it was the opposite) and then they acted like they had to unleash ten types of pestilence on me because they decided that they were the *high priestesses*, whose function was to *torment*! And they attacked my butthole with burning dart lasers, so if it hit your flesh, it could make your flesh swell up to double and quadruple mainly at your butthole.

As I consider myself a new age healer, I used lots of oil and massaged the thorny proton particles out of the butthole that resulted in the deflation of the swelling, mostly. But my clothing definitely had more add-ons of different textured clothes to layer.

But then the deviants made sure that they began hitting my eye with more precision-based lasers, hoping to at least nuclear burn one eye, if not both. As I reapplied the sour cream and other emollients on it, the eye became better. But recovery certainly was slowed down by the assaults on my hips, my facial cheekbones, my scalp, and my left shoulder blade (which connects to my heart with muscle tissue as well as blood vessels), which was repeatedly targeted, causing for my pectoral muscles to clamp up. And only when I massaged my pectorals over and over, until the popping sound released much of the static, was I able to ease into my rib cage movement. Each time I did any work, my hands that I used to type with, to write, to vigorously self-massage, to cook food, to clean up my itty-bitty apartment, to repair things, and also to use apps on my android, well my useful hands were repeatedly attacked at the veins and wrist muscles.

In addition, my ears were messed with so that my eardrums would be painful, and my nose was continually targeted until I was blowing out blood from my nostrils. My breasts were laser targeted over and over because people felt that I had acquired a fuller shape. Then my upper arms and elbows as well as ankles and feet were targeted, especially my big toe, hoping that if it would bleed at the nail, then I would be unable to walk. And repeated treatments from the doctor would cause for me to be considered a sick unit, and I'd be given euthanasia in a hurry.

And if these were the ten curses that were supposed to be hurled at me, then one must question the mental state of these despicable deviants.

Clearly, all this intense targeting of me is being considered fruitless and pointless, knowing that my final destination is Nome, Alaska. And everybody knows that I do not want to go there as a sick unit. I would like to get there while I am still healthy and can travel in comfort. My plan is—once I do get into Nome, only then can I truly meditate and pass on peacefully, by being in sync with Mother Nature.

So all in all, *more* than ten parts of my body were targeted, including my lungs, because the main deviants decided that if I had a spirituality to me, then they wanted to flaunt their norms and practices at me to show that they had a spirituality too. And that was how they decided that they just had to put me through ten tests of pestilence (and then they *exceeded* their own count of ten) just to see if they could hinder my soul's progress.

My constant response was, "No more religious persecution or persecution of any kind. We've got to stop these demonic people from beating on us while using religion as a platform!"

It is one thing for deviants to have an extreme form of a belief system regarding their personal religious norms and practices. And if they contain their practices to where it applies to them and does not endanger society, then nobody is going to give them a hard time in USA. But their relentless goal of tormenting me has truly been a blasphemy of human rights. They're using religion in a cowardly and phony way to beat up a good soul.

Some say that attending masses make guardian angels help you. And silence definitely helps you collect yourself. There are also morning spirits, afternoon spirits, evening spirits, twilight spirits, and night spirits. But nothing seems to calm these deviants down. It appears that they are too far gone. Hopefully, they might decide to direct their prayers to some positive entity.

CHAPTER 5

THE RECOVERY PHASE

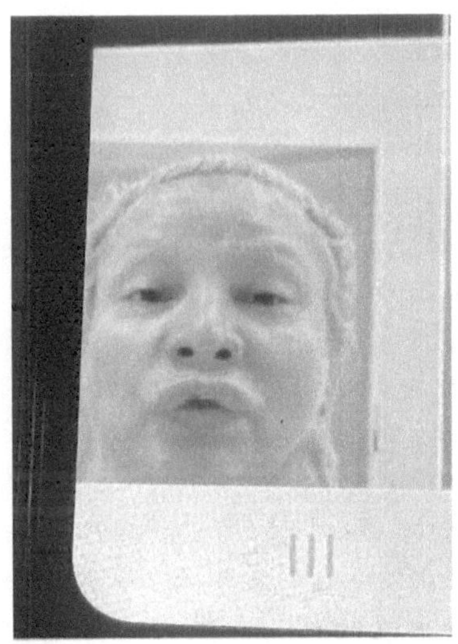

It is no secret that although I did want to save some assorted and peripheral deviants, I gave up on improving the mindset of the family vendetta deviants of India basically when they kept wanting to inflict suffering on me in a senseless way.

Even Buddhism, which originated in India, explains how suffering can be alleviated. The four noble truths clearly state the following:

1. Suffering is the essence of the world.
2. Every suffering has a cause.
3. Suffering can be extinguished.
4. It can be achieved by following madhyam marg/middle path.

But these family vendetta deviants are extremists, and they did not want to partake in any middle path behavior. And they taunted me by saying that they were beating on me because they needed to get some religious instruction from me! So again I pointed them to the Eightfold Path that are the following:

1. Right view
2. Right intention
3. Right speech
4. Right action
5. Right livelihood
6. Right mindfulness
7. Right effort
8. Right concentration

I am aware that we have to study the origins of a person from an anthropological standpoint because we cannot understand them without an understanding about where and how they were created. And I certainly understood that a lot of the deviant vendetta families of India had hoodwinked the Whites for centuries with their fake pathos and from holding a lot of exemplary Whites as hostages. That way they were able to get through lifetimes by passing off other people's productivity as their own.

As I sifted through material from different periods of history, I felt that a certain amount of healing was taking place. I was quite inspired by *The Tudors*; the fact that they could role-play just to demonstrate how danger and jealousy could topple honor and perseverance and kindness and mercy. I reflected on how I could make friends with time and paradigms, and it also occurred to me that perseverance in conjunction with desire could overcome all obstacles.

As I kept finding the golden thread of truth and many possibilities and solutions to the turmoil we face, I started to feel a lightness in my soul.

Most people want to enjoy the delights of heaven in advance. But to be in heaven, you have to obey the laws of God. Supposedly, nobody has found the location of the Garden of Eden although the Garden of Eden is where our conversation with God began and where the presence of God dwells.

We know that suffering comes from desire, but the middle path is the path to take where you should have some desire but in moderation and base your life on perseverance, compassion, virtue and wisdom.

Some say the mandate from heaven is with China. Others say that the mandate got suspended. I just know that if the majority of people in any country observe the ethics that they claim they live by, then the country's spiritual vibration is heightened. That will definitely result in getting the mandate from heaven.

So I noticed that the spirit world only helped you if you already knew the subject matter or the task at hand. Over the years, as I was evading people who were stalling me, I began to tackle my fears. For instance, my fear of gourmet cooking was erased with a bunch of new appliances. Suddenly, the confidence of being able to manage and handle a kitchen resulted in a glow that seemed to emanate from me. Also, when it came to home repairs and inventory, jotting down guidelines certainly made things more bearable.

Currently, my objective is to get past needs, to where everything is based on desire. And if my desire is reasonable and in moderation, then there's a good possibility that I won't get played like a rookie pawn. Mainly, nothing should feel like work. So if there's only lift energy and no drag energy, then most of the month should go by smoothly. Although there will always be those couple of days a month when things feel dreary. However, if there are no fatigue-filled activities, then maybe my soul will keep feeling the lightness that I do believe I have earned.

Now I'd like to have a portable workstation so I can move it around to avoid the bad energy and keep moving the workstation till

I find the good energy spot of the day/hour and mark that spot so I can build at that exact spot every day. I'd also like to be able to shower off at a moment's notice, get in my vehicle, and drive away, just so the awful spirits that have been invoked/summoned by troublemakers do understand that I am out of their range.

Sadly, it was heart-wrenching when I would have to scream my lungs out like a banshee as a reaction of the reverse polarity aimed at my lungs, but the good thing that came out of it was that after every demonic assault that was directed by the deviants onto me, I began to assess how I could have countered the black magic on me at different stages of my life.

For instance, it occurred to me that while I was a flight attendant, I could have put all my notes under different topics in separate three ring binders, especially my gliding notes. I should have maintained my daily diary on the same day even before I went to sleep and updated the names of current list of cabin crew in my logs instead of just focusing on jotting down the allowance money and the days/dates of the flights. I should have had a daily ritual that was totally foolproof, whether I was flying or relaxing, during my time off. I certainly should have held on to my hotshot camera to take initial photos, until I was able to shop for a better one. Lastly, I should have planned my clothes for the week and for each flight in detail, to make sure that there were no last-minute boo-boos.

As I began to collect myself together so I would feel less fragmented, I also rooted for a lot of people who had different obstacles than me because I realized that they wanted me to share my light with them just by addressing their issues in a compassionate way.

So I definitely spoke up about how people who live their life through psychics and clairvoyants and numerology and astrology should not be scoffed at as long as they are not breaking the law. The reason is there are many people who cannot trust their own family or their rolodex of friends, and therefore, a good psychic might be their only shot at getting an objective assessment and some decent advice. I also addressed adultery in a new way. If you look under the number 11 in chapter 8, you'll know that I want to help sex addicts find a way to blend their sex addiction in an acceptable format and get with mainstream society.

Now we all know that numerology is a very powerful science, and numbers come with a certain meaning. We also know there are people who will not do anything except on prime number days because that feels normal to them. Then there are others who will look at the movements of the planets and check their astrological houses for insights into their problems. And I certainly have put the word out that people should tolerate each other's ways of being.

Part of my recovery process also included trying to get in touch with five hundred saints, especially on All Saint's Day. Now not every saint was sensitive to my specific situation. But the seven saints that seemed in sync with me were the following:

1. St. Germain
2. St. George
3. St. Gabriel
4. St. Gregory
5. St. Thomas Moore
6. St. Ambrose
7. St. Basil

CHAPTER 6

DEAL-CHANGING GO-TOS—A-Z

On those crises-filled days when the foggy brain syndrome is on the rise, then this chapter is a good one to turn to and find something that'll work for you, just the same as chapter 8 dealing with deeds—where you can also jot down your own additional deeds that will transport you through multitudes of unfocused days. It's a good way to end a bad spell or a hex.

Anything can happen on moonless nights or day thirty-one.

Apocalypse sun goes black. Moon goes red.

Better to get anywhere approximately twenty-five minutes early.

Book of life—if your name isn't there, you are in the fires of hell.

Don't let the stigma of anything you didn't do settle upon you.

Don't bond without your prerequisite checklist or the spirit of that occasion will hold you to that moment. It is prudent to not put extra emotional energy into something that is transient.

Don't antagonize the locals if they borrow your stuff.

Don't come out at sunrise or sunset or you'll become part of the city unless you want to become part of the city.

Eat your food right after you cook it while it still has strength.

Exact prayers and invocations to fully connect.

Evil eye is a look, a stare that brings bad luck.

For martial arts, you need meditation training. Meditate till you can see the third eye and until it becomes brighter and brighter and then the four-point eye vision will happen organically.

Gold utensils attract better souls from the light.

Good ideas are fleeting. Therefore, it's best to label them.

Greater than a king is a hero; a hero fights for everyone. A king only fights for his crown.

gather, shape, design, and polish

harvest by August 27th

Have a quiet look in the truth mirror before you leave home and after you get back. Use it as a log, and be careful of the hurry demon and the pandemonium demon, which is the place of all demons.

Impeccable grooming starts the magic. So polish different routines and put them together.

It is sensible superstition to cover the mirror, so when somebody dies, their spirit will move on if they can't see their own reflection.

It is my understanding that theater is really a tool for the following:

1. *to invoke the gods,*
2. *awaken people in power without making it personal,*
3. *rehearse for your next life, and*

4. *experiment with new concept.*

Praying with a healer is good.

Photo of somebody recently deceased can be stuck on the mirror. It may give you a chance to communicate and reconnect with them.

Not about a potion and a spell and all will be well, instead sometimes it's about asking, "Is this Opposite Day?"

Questions I have:

1. So Golgotha was the hill of the skulls where the Romans crucified people. Is Calcutta a parallel to Golgotha?
2. So the Rotunda was supposedly where the tomb of Jesus is. At the Capitol building, what lies under the Rotunda?
3. So Mesopotamia is the area of modern Iraq. Is Iraq where the Garden of Eden is?
4. So does Beelzebub live in a pub?

To counter black magic, you don't necessarily have to get shamans in your home all the time. For instance, the removal of dirt spells can easily be done with a vacuum, mop, and broom or just take a long shower.

Stand with your profile to the dead body so it may not hover to you.

Sex on the bed of a witch equals death.

St. Bridget's deceased husband wanted her to offer masses for a year to help him from purgatory to heaven.

take care of anything new within forty-eight hours

The three graces—elegance, beauty, and love of life—are to be welcomed until they become part of you.

The truth in your mind should be pretty close to the truth in your heart.

You should feel like you're watching sunsets for clarity on old issues. And sunrises should spontaneously happen for new ideas and inspiration.

You should feel no strangeness when you enter a room. Instead, it should feel familiar or comfortable or you should get up and leave.

Your destiny guides your fortune or your fortune guides your destiny. Know the difference.

CHAPTER 7

GETTING TO WESTERN ALASKA

So the hard evidence that I presented via my tweets and posts didn't help my status in Anchorage all that much, but everyone knew that I was a legitimate source of knowledge. However, very few people had come up to me and said, "Thank you for all that you're doing."

As always, there are people who want to keep me in a state of torment and torture till it is time to put me in front of a camera and then they hope that they'll get to body-shame me and face-shame me. By the grace of God, they got stalled quite a bit but I do have some wounds. I'm positive that once this book is published, I shall be free from the burdens of Dharma (duty); and because I've already worked out my karma, I can go on to the next level. Aside from that, I can only say that is a good thing for an enlightened soul such as myself to write meaningful books.

Northwest of Anchorage is Nome. And Northwest of Athens is Delphi, the site of the oracle of Apollo. Through the ages, it was considered important to seek advice from the gods about the vital affairs of state. Apparently, Delphi is considered to be at the center of the world. And it is the sanctuary of Apollo.

Now I don't need to inhale vapors coming out of the ground and speak in a trance to literally be considered the oracle. All I can say is as long as there's order and cleanliness around me, the wisdom of the gods will flow through me as I am a pure instrument. Science can only answer some questions but not every question. However, there's an explanation for everything surreal if you can find the time to find it.

The year 2022 is a very crucial for many people including myself. I have decided that around the time of my birthday, November 30, 2022, I will be vigilant and observe the signs around me. There are many who feel that I should be careful and refrain from talking to just anyone randomly. I know I'd like to observe people through my peephole first, if possible, or from behind my sunglasses and then wave to them to come closer should they be nonthreatening and want feedback from me.

And if they come from abusive cults, I shall demand to know why exactly should I believe that their questions and expectations will be reasonable. Based on their miserable track record so far, shouldn't I make sure that a 110–170 ft distance is maintained at all times?

In all honesty, I envision the final chapter of my life to be amazing where drums and trumpets and a harp and ukulele are playing and a 110-gun salute sends me straight to God.

Because my thesis is—it's the beating of odds that is really indicative of the divine miracle. Once there's a miracle, you can figure out where God's presence is the strongest in your life. The human mind does have power to unleash miracles because there is a deep connection between faith and healing. So miracles start in your mind unless somebody defeats you mentally. And miracles give us hope instantly.

I had been warned in the late 90s that the path to the Source of the Light is far from paved. And yes, I did end up feeling like a voice in the wilderness. And moving towards the light as a solitary artist, rather early in my life, did feel like I was in unchartered waters, but there was no doubt in my mind that I was meant to move towards the light.

And each time I was betrayed by a lot of very manipulative people, God was the only constant. And it was a natural progression in my relationship with God to know that there was nothing else on this planet that matters as much as God does.

So it follows that courageous, true seekers will get a proper chance to cocreate with the God of Light and write out their own destiny that should blend in with God's plan.

I have scrutinized my incident logs carefully, and the records indicate that my life was saved time and again by heavenly powers. What I'm describing could possibly be at least three miracles. Oh, and I did not base that on some solitary half-baked incident. I think I measured up really well by any paranormal standards.

There are nonbelievers who have been known to ask God to get them out of hopeless situations, and they have succeeded. But to keep those channels of communication open for good, they might want to be in sync with God. Because God is beyond imagination. God is invisible, intangible, but just know that we can definitely sense God. And if we look for physical manifestations of God, we will surely find it. It's in the timing though.

CHAPTER 8

DDDD

11 11 44 44

11 *Dictums*

1. Thou shall refer to 11 11 44 44 daily, work on it, and polish it.
2. Thou shall respect time, and thou shall not be late.
3. Thou shall perform well thy earthly duties—doctor, plumber, architect, firing squad.

4. Thou shall obey the law of the land.
5. Thou shall honor thy father and mother to the extent that they're honorable.
6. Thou shall not steal. (Food is an excusable exception in an emergency.)
7. Thou shall not kill unless thou art a soldier/executioner in compliance with your ethics and code of conduct.
8. Thou shall not bear false witness (unless thou are a pure saint and lie by omission for the greater good in apocalyptic times).
9. Thou shall do onto others as you would have them do onto you (based on hierarchy of merit and job title).
10. Thou shall not have or worship harmful deities (i.e., demons).
11. Thou shall not commit adultery (unless in a sex fest with at least eight witnesses or four in an emergency).

11 *Demerits*
(listed L–R from full-blown to miniscule)

1. arrogance/pride/snobbery/vanity
2. vendetta/revenge/violence/power struggle
3. rage/anger/disdain
4. betrayal/lies
5. rape/lust
6. sloth/lazy/procrastination/pending
7. greed/gluttony/hoarder
8. jealousy/envy/lack
9. hate/despise
10. despair/hopeless/helpless/fear
11. delusions/addictions (sex, gambling, substance abuse, daydreaming, self-pity)

44 *Disciplines*

1. loyalty

2. family/bloodline honor (where your word is your bond)
3. honesty/truth
4. frugality
5. manual n menial tasks
6. perseverance/patience
7. wisdom/prudence
8. humility/humble speech
9. diligence/duty
10. morality (based on archetype)
11. ethics (based on profession)
12. compassion/empathy
13. generosity/mercy
14. courage
15. martial arts as defense
16. cleanliness/neatness
17. leadership/responsibility
18. chastity/purity
19. peacefulness/calmness
20. discernment/logic
21. love/tolerance
22. forgiveness (based on reality, not delusions)
23. temperance/ balance
24. higher education/evolution
25. faith/hope
26. brevity/wit
27. perfection/posture
28. righteous justice/due process
29. promptness/instantly
30. travel
31. visionary
32. progress
33. total mind-body synchrony
34. pure desire in moderation
35. liberty/freedom enhancer
36. devotion
37. constance/consistent

38. pinpoint
39. professional courtesy
40. proven paradigms inventor
41. observation and researching
42. hosting and entertaining
43. Hoh
44. inspiring ethical leader/spiritual leader

44 Deeds
(guidelines to add on merits)

1. how to pack/unpack
2. how to cook
3. how to clean
4. how to shop
5. sailor
6. pilot
7. astronomer
8. engineer/architect
9. public speaking
10. sing
11. dance
12. host/showstopper
13. piano
14. harp
15. ukulele
16. drums
17. accounting and bookkeeping
18. filing and typing
19. bartender
20. gardener
21. lifeguard
22. Girl Scout
23. paralegal
24. driver
25. healer masseuse

26. herbs and aromatherapy
27. vibrational frequencies
28. crystals
29. French/Latin
30. Italian
31. Russian
32. Swiss
33. calligraphy
34. sketching
35. painting
36. caricature
37. swimming
38. pony back riding
39. skating
40. skiing
41. tennis
42. ping-pong
43. baseball
44. basketball

In addition to the *4 Ds (dictums, demerits, disciplines, and deeds)*, it is important to note that just by observing *order and time* and through getting the house spirits to be on your side, you can minimize the collision course with the dark side should you choose to do so. Also, by getting closer to the light, using generosity of spirit, you can ask heavenly beings to strengthen you and to break all chains and bonds that bind you. Especially if your chains and bonds weren't through your own shortcomings.

You will also know if the light is working for you when things line up organically. For instance, I've always wanted to have specific and pertinent information at my fingertips, anytime, anywhere; and sometimes when it happens, I know that the laws of synchronicity are working for me.

'Those who wish to rise in their spirituality can set spiritual goals for themselves while reading the chapter dealing with 11 11 44 44. Then they can decide in a BID WHIST/RUMMY way to project just how many points (hands) they can strive to make. And based on their bid, we will know which level of spirituality they are aspiring to in a realistic way. A good/above average bid, in my opinion would total to at least 7 7   11   11 out of the 11   11   44   44 guide-lines that I have put out there for the spiritually curious.'

ABOUT THE AUTHOR

My totem energy is playful, but I have an acute sense of good ethics and values. I like making friends with professionals mainly. I value kindness, hard work, vision, integrity, and punctuality. I have to polish a lot of aspects of mine in the category of *deeds*, and I plan on doing that the moment I am free of my tormentors.

I look forward to moving to a more peaceful chapter of my life.